THE PACIFIC NORTHWEST POETRY SERIES

THE BOOK OF MEN AND WOMEN

Poems by David Biespiel

University of Washington Press   *Seattle & London*

The Book of Men and Women, the ninth book in the
Pacific Northwest Poetry Series, is published with
the generous support of Cynthia Lovelace Sears.

© 2009 by the University of Washington Press

Printed in the United States of America

Design by Ashley Saleeba

12 11 10 09   5 4 3 2 1

University of Washington Press

P.O. Box 50096, Seattle, WA 98145 U.S.A.

www.washington.edu/uwpress

Library of Congress Cataloging-in-Publication Data
Biespiel, David, 1964–
The book of men and women : poems / by David Biespiel.
p. cm. — (Pacific Northwest poetry series ; 9)
ISBN 978-0-295-98914-3 (alk. paper)
I. Title.
PS3552.I374B66 2009
811'.54—dc22   2008054126

The paper used in this publication is acid-free and 90 percent
recycled from at least 50 percent post-consumer waste. It meets
the minimum requirements of American National Standard for
Information Sciences—Permanence of Paper for Printed Library
Materials, ANSI Z39.48-1984. ∞

FOR STANLEY PLUMLY

No one knew me under the mask of similarity, nor even knew that I had a mask. . . . No one imagined that at my side there was always another, who was in fact I. They always supposed I was identical to myself.

—FERNANDO PESSOA, *The Book of Disquiet*

Look as your looking-glass by chance may fall,
Divide, and break in many pieces small,
And yet shows for the selfsame face in all . . .

—MICHAEL DRAYTON, "Verses Made the Night Before He Died"

CONTENTS

THE BOOK OF MEN AND WOMEN

EVENING WATCH

Now I see the eggish waves
Hatching beneath the geese.
Now the risk of love
Comes back and moves
The crises from this face.

A talon's clutch of sugar,
An hour of stale loss,
All the kid stuff to bear
And wiser ways
Of introducing fear—

None of it like this moon—
Or one-eyed holy men.
You sleep. You sleep and soon
The shabby chill is gone
And the illumination.

I think of no rationale—
Though maps perish,
And passers-by turn cruel
And become invisible—
To justify a wish.

The light has oversold this wound.
You sleep, you turn. The air
Wheels out and mills around
The room—like proof—then bends
Perversely to the floor.

You sleep, you turn. The shadows
Don't hide dangers, or wrongs.
And standing here can't do
Away with dark—nor
Span the wan-ness of a man.

1

GENESIS 12

That night, in the trustless summer wandering out of that country
As if cursed by a nation, I settled in and slept like a seed.
The air knuckled through the tent, and the old muses, suspended
With regret and grief in dream, were foggy as a tumult of trees.
And the leaves were gotten souls. And the damp light was a fair
      woman.
And the ultimatums in my heart, and the kindred bleating of sleepers,
Were small candles of serenity—and all the while the riverless land
      back there
Near my father's house was lifting out of my mind like a fallow prayer.
There was love, too, sure—my wife, yes, my sister. And there was flight
And blessings of breaking into wishes and silence.
Once, when you came back from the other bed, wasted as death,
I ached heavy as rotten fruit and vowed into the new land—
Such serious joy I haven't found on this journey yet, not once, not
In this desert or in the old one, not under stars of promises or
      forewarned
God be with us crying. I'm certain I've lost my mind.

POET AT FORTY

When have I last doubted the tawdry and the weird

Or the dry ploys that only the gravel blind could love?

The weather-beaten I once called *beauty*, the brunt of worrying

That's never shaken—are these the jitters or a slow burn?

Even the flattered are dogs now. Sure, that ravishing Star of David

Couldn't be more dreary—nor supping with the impish stem-winders
     and swingers.

That's why I crib this guesswork and shim and detail

A tonnage of mannerism into a hunger for the fusty.

Restrained, birth-marked, cast off, I didn't stake out a beggar's
     prophecy.

Instead, I hunker and doze with the late impatiens,

And, like a keeper of reveries, I tally the rings of their ripening pallor.

THOUGH YOUR SINS BE SCARLET

It didn't start with the phenobarbitol or the reefer,
The ironweed or the magnetic force of a gentle woman.
It started with a voice saying *return* that I could not hear,
And the nineteen *amidahs* did nothing for transgressions.
Scarletted-up—all those years—I fiddled and giggled
And got muscle-bound as a deaf dreamer, a striper,
A pressed-against pirate, got teary and ripe with the scuttled
Worry coming back again and again, and no winners
To speak of, no vintage TV to settle in with like sins
Of the zodiacal light or kissing cousins or crummy laws.
I haven't been called a weak sister, and I don't mean to, that's plain.
But the rummy tumblers, the bloody knuckles, I'll crawl
For them. I'll crawl. And the cutting up and the swear words—
Such crimson no wool can wrap around. Look unto the lampblack
And see givers and campy gents and you'll forgive anything hard.
I have. Remember? It was just after she left, burning the last wick.

THE EX-LOVERS CLOSE DOWN THE HAWTHORNE BOULEVARD BARS ON THE 1000TH NIGHT OF THE WAR

In this city of puddles they smirk and roam, boast and weep. Their
       gobbledy-gook is as good as code,
Their names retrofitted with fear, their condition all headache.
There are parables for this behavior, a proper blab, and none more
       rapacious, none more true
Than the teary king, his picture hanging from the billboards and
       bridges. The teary king,
Divine, jacked-off, peevish, unharmed, like a hideous garden heavy
       with lavender.

Most nights they're livid. They're lifters. They pilfer and dance with
       stern faces, cagey
With their suckled scat, unshaken by the drill, until the cask goes
       bottoms-up.
That's when they go starkly through the streets and play their dark
       bodies like cards
And frighten themselves—he with his mopey joy, she with her long
       braids,
Their lappets dragging in the gutters, as they dart in the alleys like
       botched and dreamy punks.

EMBOUCHURE

1

Here's a peek-a-boo at my feather-light upkeep:
I'm pickled as a lost keepsake—and, dear, I say to myself, dear,
You're a sub-man, a busy mass.
You have a lush noose draped over your ears. Call it field armor.
And the way you lord it on with your desperate scrub,
Chucked, mauled, like a morality play—
With your cluttered lookout and holy occult, pooled
For the next torment—is brighter than a groomsman's hickey.
Where are the moors when you want to sprawl in your sore wreckage
And back into the gaffe of a good pint?
What's the mileage on the inescapable ship in that bottle?

2

Beneath winter's dark pizzazz and beneath the few starlings' zippered
        reaction times,
Beneath the dewy light, and despite the beaten, months-old "Merry
        Christmas" colors,
I stand and manage to hear the New Year's geese
And notice the twin yellow roses over the fence.
I stand, meek and garbled, firing off my riffs.
And despite the unsureness of my chops, my head
Is no better for being stewed into the wee-er hours.
No better than being rebuffed by love.
(And the little uncertainties, hesitations, of my desire, and the
        enormous uncertainties,

Like the interior scaled-down cartography of a heart, these I've sought
        to stiff-arm and send off.)
I've met what was necessary, like a sentry for pinpoint sighing,
Met what was sensual in the muskegs, in the sedge and scummy bogs,
Met the crass and the dead and the orthodox pantheists
Who are impious and stammer
With their forgotten IOUs (they are so beautifully jowled, like Jews).
And I've met what was unnecessary: the smarmy master-at-arms,
The tarred-and-feathered trusts, the drawn bridges, the vacant
        party-boats.
There was no karmic trickster among that lot.
And now as the wind picks up like a distant thought, I understand that
        what I once had—
Guts, for instance, or forbearance, rebelliousness—
Hasn't come home in some time.
I know that before I discover such neat objects as better wine
And learn the sweeter tunes to blow over the tops of the three-quarter-
        empty bottles,
A lulling tune or a fleshy tune,
Tunes for the meeting houses and the strongest shoulders and
        the feet of the poor and the forgers and threaders,
Tunes for the darker brains and the rumpled beds of lovers
And the months of cursed rain,
Only then can I get back into shape, with the brunt of my corks trailing
        behind me.

KOHAIN

I came over like a fool, pilfering the shells from parables, a fellow
      of the inbred drink, my duh tonic.
The idée fixe, an edited riff, was fair. Efficiently I came over, and
      handing back the covenant like a coin—
I got out of the temple right before the *aliyahs* got given,
Initiated, tizzied, unself-helped, cool-headed, pampered, conventional
      as italicized palmistry.
Then the road was a repeating panorama, and anything narrow
      preened like fire,
And the ale was fine, and there was no rotgut.
The tiller steered right to the sun's idiot veil. I came over and wasn't
      burned—
Having left the velvet intimacies and enduring handshakes to become
      grist for junk,
Dancing at the city gate in my borrowed coat,
Staging my *midrash* for the stars, like an outlaw in love with disgust.
That night: The autumn breeze embroidered the streets with broken
      loves.
And the birds seemed hand-knitted in the branches.
And the sky ached with its dark horse.
And though I clearly knew the star-systems, I chose the orphan's court
Over the clubby, the chanters, and come-home dogs.
And all along, my muscle memory was no good: I'd think *loam*, but I'd
      say *muck*.

THE SLEEPING BEAUTY

She likes it back there, spell-bound and rubbed smooth,
Without a substitute or any lingerer to listen in to her weariness
(She's a maharani, ransacked as a house). And the harness of dream,
        and the error of disappearance
Are normal, newsless, shining even, cadenced as a dance, swank.

And though she seeps like a suicide and can't replenish the color
        of raw,
Her parted erasure is an intricate solitude, edgy and scrubbed, like
        undergrowth,
So that the error of one's looking on dissolves her spirits.
And the clarity of what some called her hiccups, the cadaverous
        coughs—

These are the intimacies of the houseflies that rise and fall and strafe
        around her.

DOVER BUTCH

This cliffside is true and ruthless and dependable—
What all the pundits say is right: you can dabble
With love, you can plead, but the bitter, etc., isn't lucrative.
The bitter, etc., is borrowed, marriageable. And the waves
Don't sound any more mournful than a woman—
Besides all the perfumed armies are so grumpy and wan
And blotto you'd think they couldn't keep up with their Sophocles
Even at a snail's pace—such dense, ancient sadness.
Yes, faith must be called to, fat with spray and misery,
Though nothing there is crumbling. Sure, I can channel the
     calm sea
So that the moon is my darling, my orbit, my omphalos—
And yet it's nothing to get rattled by. Try humming at a window.
Such is this children's game, such is this mother's tongue.
Who says my girdle's too tight? My heart is flung.

CITIZEN DAVE

Now that we are sending him out of the chorister and into the clarity
      of grief,
He's no longer at risk of being so stuck up. He's all country folk now,
      aloof
As a tunnel, passable, a sap. He's less prodigy, more Junior,
Less doggy, more half-caste. If a glowing God turned him out poor
He'd pucker up to the lag line—negligent and lame—and forgive
      nothing.
He's no mahatma—his theme is mayhem. He wags
His credit just the same at dilettantes as revved-up ladies—
There'll be no one to piss in his ear when his brain's on fire. Today
He nabs one last vote and debates the future of agog—
Still, he's gotten murky or redemptive, and his fangs are gone.
The sight of the sun going down leaves him strangely overjoyed.
He's a goner, tapered, setting out for silence, and no good.

TALE BEARER

Some day I will go back to where that thoroughfare begins, and the
      thieves are gruff
With their rich hats, and the terrazzo is rich, and to hurtle in any
      direction
Is to know that flat country as a ream of stammerers and crooners.

And I will rejoin those players, and we'll be starry-eyed and natty with
      our vagrant navigations
And our smoky yap, uncorking our stop volleys,
Risking the seminal reverbs, blaspheming.

That's how wormy it once was, with morsels of daisies and a leg
      up at the zero hour.
Some were ordinary seamen, some sounders, but all could, like
      a season, affect a manner
Of the musty (dormant as rain). We were deans of the snide, sarcastic
      as oracles,

Semi-lunar, self-surveying, sated with our tinny boxcar traits, and fêted.
We held the crown and tit and zippers of bad love. Our tales unhappy
      with freedom.
Then, stripping for a mate, as if home were all languor and barter, we
      shuddered and grew silent.

2

MISSISSIPPI GOD DAMN

Here in this strumming light which the generations can't downshift
　　　out of,
And with the land gushing its courtesies of iron, and the shallow
　　　mercies
Caustic or strangely gussied up like dogs with dark collars, I lose
　　　my rest.
And what druthers I had are just trouble now, unconditional, all
　　　in the air.
What's got me upset are the dead. They go too slow. They're
Just plain rotten—even a beating heart hardly tingles.
The crimes, the land, the lost second sight, the prayers—
None of these are picking the cotton out of the lies.
And no banter between the roots and the tombs.
And no thoughts boycotting the feelings. The old rooms,
The shadow towns, the rebel yelling, the Confederate daughters,
And the themes of homesteads get hushed in the months-long heat.
I've gotten too damn lazy to pluck a duplicate heart,
Unearth a body, a song, an I-just-don't-know-what kind of fly.
That's just the trouble—the genie's not gentle, the stomach
Can't stomach the risk of being right, good, unknown, me.
And if I race to the dry river where the bodies are pushing through,
The bones peering like children from behind a curtain of dirt, then
　　　who
Shall judge the living? And if that's a test what frown is needed,
What game face does everybody know to put on? What hoof? What
　　　blood?

RICHARD HUGO

Lately I've been thinking about bridges and brides,

Blacks and Jews. All that can explode.

Not like a factory, I'm thinking of, from years ago, blasted

On some cockeyed moonlight run over Slovakia.

But still, what's forbidden, chastened, seduced, though even that
      gets old

As a preacher jawboning in his riverside motel.

There's no ghetto to luxuriate in here. Without it, what's to pity?

Lately I've been thinking about the bits of glass I saw in Coos Bay,

About poverty and solidity or what one once loved

About territories of migrants, semi-pro ball,

The scorched and unforeseen, and obedient,

The bells, birds, and tractors,

About drinking songs, hymns, and long roads,

Grebes and greenhorns, tragedies and grim grass.

Things happen, it's said, dignified, bloody, or insufficient.

And the *If nots* don't add up the winnings. And the odd creatures are
      cordoned off

Like contraband. And the pools are closed.

And the police gallop by with their hungry dogs.

The victorious wives, the vices of college kids, new mail, the rhymes of
      the knowing:

These are dealt with in museums, frozen like pioneer dioramas.

And yet to seize the day with a long-neck

Still sounds good to mothers at home in their thick rooms—

Scouring the stew—unrescued.

OLD ADAM OUTSIDE THE WALL OF EDEN

How many times have I come to renew this pre-Fall Diaspora with
      its Alpha flavors
And filial lyres, as if looking at wind and autumn linnets?
The stone wall is still here, untranslatable. And the chuckleheads,
      for example,
Are still chewy as dashes. They only understood the purity of the
      over-measure,
The clues of scalding left on the foreskins of madmen, and on
      occasion—
Though it requires that they hunker behind their weather-beaten
      peltas—they still try
To how-do-you-do. For them, it's put-and-take. For me, mordent,
      rejoined,
I'm still gerrymandering my nadir. That lyric in my head
Is hotter than fire in a dog's mouth.

There are times, though this isn't one of them, when I'm closer to hip
      and unredeemed,
When, on the other side of here, the chitter torments my ideals,
Slung, as they are, in a game of dodge and slip.
There are times when spot work is all I have (I can grunt like any
      Prussian bricklayer).
Gooey, dicey, monomial, roly-polial, and pall-borne:
These days I lie flat on the sands as if floating into a lease of
      noiselessness
And think of her shushing me on the sifted path. Then our future:
A rocky torque, a crazed streak, plenty of Hizzoners to go around.
We saw nothing but pitch. Our rein state was impossible.

But seeing these stars, from any promontory or seaside—as if just
  seeing was a tool for hope—
Seeing these stars was home enough (it couldn't cure my melancholia
  or break up
Malcontent waves, but it was precious).
Surely they were life, unpardoned, endearing,
Rising overhead like a truce.
Even the rills of the moon seemed godly. And the absent tides
Coming in and out, in and out, catapulted and unhampered,
Glossed over like a lost synapse,
Great tides that I believe I swam in as if in the grave: my cadence, my
  lullaby.

GENESIS 27

—Isaac

And the tent stood in darkness, with the dew, and the curses.

And the blessings sung and spit at, longed-for, won over—

Like the smells of fields I drew joy from—all that fatness

And smooth-skinned stink and the moths at the flaps

With their horns of judgment, I couldn't get their gutted pitch out
       of my ear.

What vow has my tongue rotted? Who is the foe, the deceiver, but
       my self?

Truly, my people have become such a host for wars. I think of smoke
       when I think.

So I try not to think and sit up for the next feeding, blind, skimmed,

And wagging *Your Excellency* at the God-awful moon.

Still, the surge of death, and the dot of death, are not kind to me.

OVERCAST

The sky's soft focus was steadfast, like ice fog, touched-up as a fossil or
      foul-mouthed sparrow—
Its solo a melee, a pastoral point of honor, and whorled as a riverhead.
We lived the war out in that light. Under the river trees,
Rocks and semolina-colored roots.
Under our canonicals, the cool, slick contractions of the clan.

And in summer the canopy of luck brought on doubt and old-school
      double-standards
We couldn't shake off, couldn't bring our best gamesmanship to
      (though we could be pampered
In a gallery of smidgens, dreaming).
It was all so Late Latin—the lead-off tableau and the letter-perfect
      talent.
We gave up addressing our own consciousnesses and embraced the
      paved city.

And then it was afternoon. The cedar waxwings were tipped-off in
      a panic.
The spirit in the streets was triumph, devotion,
Gold dust, endless talk.
Happy with disparate truths and tripe,
Suddenly, we were all free of the infighting.

And nothing but reunions, laughter (a little egocentric weeping was
      encouraged). Nothing but the finest gifts—
We passed out tam-o'shanters but never wore them afterwards.
We were masters of sham. Whether in *schul* or on Sam Hill,

Whether masquerading or sloshed

And surrendered, or true blue, we wouldn't forfeit our lives.

It was the pit of skulls that brought us satisfaction.

It was our martial timbre.

And there were no mulligans. And there were no gummed-up last
      words—the dead were not a tuning fork.

We slathered the slang on good, and glad to make a milk run when
      asked to—

That was the hybrid year, overburdened, as we were, with grim heroic
      dirty work.

And then it was evening. We rummaged through the hellboxes, among
      the hearsay

And the giddy honky-tonks. It was all a pigeon hole for a Neo-
      something:

Neo–rest home, neo-steerage, neo–ten spot. The new was our pratique,

Our trellis to the mussed-up, the moola, the ungirted, the goners,
      the gin mills.

And whatever was found in the word book, whatever was too
      ornamental to thaw,

We ticked it off (some were bitter about it),

And our new credo was to be leery, crafty, in love with blarney, balking
      at the fresh, kibitzing.

Still, no one really knew what day it was, but the long purples

Were coming up in the dark, unbaptized again, pulsating,

Half-opening, as if getting rid of faith, brimming, under the clouds.

WILLIAM CLARK'S SONNETS

DISCOVERY

We toppled ourselves, word by word, bloodied
With pronouncement. Mean, stiff: Damnation
Was good as supper. We glowed in our shattering.
But what was worthy cloyed us too (we never
Lashed ourselves, certainly). What good?
We were the flat fish emboldened to breathe.
Nothing so dire as our directive,
To dig in and credit what was true. That,
And making of the mist new nouns. Close up
The vapor was a wheeze, avian, glib.
Nothing so lovely as the fruit fly, our
Humanitarian fiefdom to come.
The nights ranted: *I could hate Man*. So we stuck
To the due given us, untrimmed, tolled.

YORK

None of us understood, really, what there was
To love. We were sabbatarians, saved
By our ninety-five theses. But York—
Unbathed, our heathen—he trudged alongside,
My man among us, jaunty as sin.
Hypocrisy was our practice, our saraband,
Our elocution, cluttering the lot.
We were the ones shackled, cut deep and locked.
But it meant nothing in the end. As for my slave,
My poltergeist, call him what you will,
I'd shuttle from flexible to feeble,
Pistol at my side. I could glitter like dust.
And my pores were incensual. Sunk or slipped,
I excerpted him with my hatchet-man of a mind.

RULE

Evenings the strange trees were inaudible.
They blended with doubt as our cadences
Were nabbed, undone, tattered, like detours.
You could order tender, end up with rut.
Out on the fields, in the bemired maybes,
I'd think of Caedmon and know that manners
Couldn't be dominant, couldn't be much
More than a living wage. Sudden hawks
Were our guffaws, all the vogue we could rustle.
And the confidential communication
Between Lewis and me, even before
The winter with the Mandans, was fermenting.
We ruled with the whip. We sauntered and were
Terrible, impish, pleased with our tempers.

FUTURE

I could've spent hours as a shepherd,
Fisherman, fireproofing my sheaves. I could've
Remained snug with my trigger, unspattered,
Grousing with brutes and guttersnipes. And all along
My pearl a Lord's Prayer of prodding, a mudless scheme
Where nothing was natural, nothing as shod
As these poor skins. —I think of it now in this unscathed light,
In the nose-blood, monkshood switch of the trail.
What's to learn again from rebuke and thunk
And sore ribs? The river that is unwritten
Is as close as a stalled wind, its dreamy mouth
Closed and breakerless. And the itinerary
Of dying is knitted into my skin like an itch.
What rebirth will there be, clothed in this endless sky?

EZRA POUND

Ninth of May, rain, and the prices are crap.
And the Indian preachers still make a good impression
On the lonely wives—this is so far from the piazzas and espressos
        (the dosage here small and black).
Nothing a banker would understand like barnstorming rebels or race
        relations.

There's little reprieve from this blare, little to splint, like a mind.
America is all markdown now, and its music full of antic scams,
And its *esprit de corps* is snagged like the national income,
And its frontiersmen are too satisfied with roughage.

In this I understand little, squeaking like an ugly cousin, pocked face,
        worse than fraternal.
It's as if failure were less fickle than I expected it to be. Courage—once
        the rage—
Is now all crank and glissando (the old courage resembled the
        nuthatch,
Hopping with chatter down the bark of the tree).

BAD MARRIAGES

Even a man who always comes home forgets the sense of it. He lets the
        halls glint with agony and pleasure.
He lets light into windows through the veils of give-and-take, lets the
        bath prick him like a thousand tacks.

In the insomniac's hour he prowls the cellar with his warrior's luck,
        smoking the birthday dope,
Smearing the irregular cave of his mind and the faces and the ticking
        clocks and the girlish thighs

He touched in a season of first love, early summer, the sky of the city
        illuminated with improvised musk, a spree of sheets,
And suddenly she's removed her dress. And suddenly the squares of
        darkness dissolve.

Even a man who can't come home looks in vain through gates of
        sporadic gardens, sacred
As dragging a leg, tormented as a rood beam, under which he
        sometimes stops and breathes

Harder than he meant to. He's a city cut in half, man on the one side,
        thorny
As rain, home on the other—

He's like a passion flower looking up
At buildings and bridges, gates and windows,

And through one he sees a closed passional
With the downcast and the sufferers and the promiscuous weariness,

And he thinks a pastry would be nice. —All of which the stoned man
  sniffs in his brain
Until the password for sleep comes on, and the stairs creak with the
  volley of his steps,

And the city of marriages collapses in ruins, and the maple volunteers
  are a light emptiness,
And the thrushes begin their early adjurations along the leaf-ruined
  gutters, July decaying like a desert of the drowned,

Drier than a complaint, ending like a book underlined in red in the
  meaningful sections,
The confused words with the clear words, *To Be Continued* with *The
  End*, enduring like a dead wind.

LUKE'S UKULELE

As the white sky crept to its benchmark beauty,
He slept most that day and made haste slowly.
And as he slept—fifteen, fretted like a candlewick,
Craggy as a frozen garden, un-guarded as a darling,
Lushly unburdened—he dreamt of abandon.
If he saw himself a straw man, he saw the woozy hours
He'd longed-and-been-done-in for—plus
The unseeded air that shucked pure wit out of the eye.
And then he saw despair—not as a housebound critter
But a beast best left to the winter hills
That chummed and swelled outside the last miles of the city.
The hills no place to travel, no place to say farewell.
Or if time has traction, if time has charms, with a jingle-jangle
And the raw, new voice, and with his songs of love and hate
And bared teeth, he can lift above what sun is left,
Lift and wane, and land far enough from men.

P.O.E.M.

—Portland Office of Emergency Management

Lately we've stored our own hearts in this cellar's safety corner,

Crooned like radio static and grew fatty with our craft.

The matches, the can openers, the ready-to-eat rice,

The blankets, candles, the gloves and duct tape: what is it all

But daft aid? Even the axes and brooms can't keep

Our cave clean or the mob at bay. And sirens that sing

"Keep your heads down." And contaminated noise

Behind the eyes—is that a warning or prior preparation?

Even the layers and years of floods or fear of dirty bombs

Has became a consciousness of maps and bottled water.

Memory is the last of the broken glass. At first we bleated

Our ditties at hard rain and belted evensongs at wind.

We lamented, serenaded, and wheezed the blues—

A shackle of laughter mixed with rye and good smokes.

But these were just madsongs, fabliaux, echoes

That droned and decontaminated nothing—

Not even rivers or the fountains—

With their repetitions and linked rhymes.

Only chanting and riddles held back the bitter words.

And what of our incantation of diminishing verse and filthy obscurities,

Our periphrasis and unending catalogues?

Little more than the blunt knack for snookering.

In the end, we survive. And instead of triumphal odes, we give in to
      counterpoint,

Squint out of our iridium shelters one morning, and resume

Our places. But first, excited about the day's cruddy air

And, as if only the unharnessed voice is left, we scream.

MASS MAN

His was the occult balance and the bunches of ploys and oblique
      blocks. He called them *my little theaters.*
And the joke books, like a cool hereafter, and the jinxed feeling he had
      just crossing the boulevard—
These he sought protection from, like a child skittish around small
      dogs.
He feared the larrup of a martinet, though none lived in his city.

Still he loved the hard pan and the form work and to mill around,
      languorous as a lamp trimmer,
In the retail shops and old movie houses. He'd sit for hours,
      harrumphing and then mum, then hurt
About his rights, in a lather about loan blends and stemwinders,
      avoiding the *minyans* and mowed lawns.
There was no way to tease the foul inflections from his mind, so he
      paired off alone, became a fluke,

Hocked his nice-nellyism, and loaded his heart against the enemies of
      the state.

3

THE HUSBAND'S TALE

I'd earned my polyglottic wounds, gold-digging, lopping off, pouring
        out the repartee —
Rattled, over-taxed, powered down then tapered, from prefab to
        repossession,
From exalted to laid low, from whippoorwill to flapper.
Shaggy, tagged, obligated, crossbred —I dogged the shoddy
Like taproots to a farrago.
And it was there, lost in a city of make-believe,
That I sought out the give-backs and dirty jeers
And gave up misbehavior and slogging and baited guilt,
Where I resisted the creepy premiums and the gimcracks,
Resisted balking at the new and the raunchy,
Clutching, instead, my comeback like cabinet wine.
But I'd grown lymphatic—my dominant method, my windowless
        stucco.
All that was left was a frail mask for staging a chronicle of shucks—
Cussed out, whup-assed, mushy, unadorned.

THE WIFE'S TALE

Now the sky, groggy and spackled, the clouds capsizing, the rain
      cleared.
These days even my hagiographies are fabrications, as are so many
      things,
Microscopic, reeking of the dismal—
Even my *kashruth* has gone bad, loopy, like a thug, a shucked
      keepsake.
It hasn't always been like this.
The corridors of smack and drunkenness are closed now.
No tad of laziness to get rattled by. My façade is all clapboard,
      a sample of crud—
Narcissistic, stagnant, deft as a destiny, a feathery vision.
And as soon as I have a leg up and grin
I become an inflationist, frail, fractioned, and crappier than a porkpie
      hat.
Hitched to that loss ratio, veiled, I leach like a slur
And piece together what I have known: a plug for secrets, a mask for
      the other things.

THE WIFE'S TALE (II)

There, where the lake breeze was recently laggard and reeked
Like gruel in a barrel, where I embraced inanition
And held no grudges with dogs nor understood the myrtle warbler's
Let-downs or mythical laws (as if such a thing can even be sutured
Or tipped off or renamed), there, my eyes were quiet as a pony's—
Though later, like tenacious cities with their reckless raving nights.
Even so, I knew to be careful as a waif—my patter song wasn't that
        naughty.
I could look at love and see a foe, or caught out
As a foe, I could see the *passe partout* of rapture.
He touched my hand just once, gentle as a game point.

THE CROONER

His self-contented days are over. And the caustic-tone rows, and the
      cave art
Ticked off with its kinetic raconteur—that's been given up too, along
      with the stylebook and the leaky boots.
Even when he thought of himself as foppish, he couldn't pilfer pride or
      give the shaft to the dead—

What he needed was a moral hazard for liquor and a light ship.
      So he mocked-up the Jovian brogue,
Reticulated the choriambs like tarnished rumbas,
And eloped into opulence.

Did he need more kerchiefs to mop up the garlands?
Even when he turns to mumbo jumbo, he gets mournful. It's
      maddening,
This measly rigmarole he's come to, this voice, his crazy quilt.

Unadvised, pleased with the take-home pay of it all, teetotaling,
He glimmers like a forgotten mouth, aims for the deep end of all that's
      muddy and dim,
And mocks the majesty of ringers. Same for the hay-high dandies.

PRUDERY

Sure, I'd binged on nibbling and trucked with an interlocutress,
ID'd the lady's thumb, been bawdy, cluttered, cuddled.
Sure, I'd sought the rudimentary detours of longing,
Thought of keepsakes and dowries and credited a fondle.
That was my binary self. A genetic mosaic, a fallacy,
As if the years there, or that one night even—lying on her bed, clothed,
      sleepless, like two tassels
Shimmering toward resistance, resisting, and at last the sun coming in,
      and her skin—
Were the good elegies for failure.

Not like the honey gilding that came later, or the glory of the hollow-
      eyed,
Not like placating the Episcopal self, the destructionist self,
The pistol-whipped, the crutched,
Shouldering the asocial self. And not like the hog-tied torque of the
      self, the practical,
The never-corrupted, that night, but a man left
Snazzy in the corner of a party with an undertow and dosage of wonder
The new scapegoat for his despair. There, my pigeonhole
For some time thereafter, posturing in my new speak, stomaching the
      table talk.

LUST

The damage begins this way: first in the lymph nodes, like a holy slice
      of lost,
Then with the precision of the pell mell, a lump that's a placebo,
Impermanent, limber. Then the problem chafes like meperidine.
No rye can correct it. Your heart scuffed, your hands scripted like place
      cards.
And the damage goes on, and without its fix of trembling you can't
      answer its pouty bell.

And the muscatel of it, the negative glow of it, the stymied
Catlike luck and glimmer of it: No toggle switch can shut them down.
They're woven like longing.
And no stoup can rectify it.
Its silk is in your blood and kindred. You can't turn it into an
      index set.

But the tentacles, the labyrinth and hammer-toe of desire overtakes
      you,
And you see that the navigations and rump lines are merciless,
Dabbled, unscripted, tied-up, self-slandered, untillable,
Like a tomahawk in your head.
You're marooned, a jack-a-dandy, piecemealed, attired for phooey,
      slinking, low-browed, and slammed.

Suddenly you feel your mouth bleat. You're over-mastered.
Suddenly you laugh in public and spasm—
And the yellow verbena you saw in the coastal dunes, where the
      unknown beloved

Is never sallow and calamity is a dream, the yellow verbena glitter like
    halos—
And if you could, you'd dive into the liquefaction of the body you
    want, far away, *terefah*.

A CLOUD OF CROWS

Tawny and winterish, and wobbly, like a wan

Spinsterish cowgirl, and tailor-made for work

Where there's a remedy for everything except death—

I saw her wind down and holler *What!*

In the glinted light that Apriled into the daffodils.

She was scrubbing brusque words onto yellow paper,

Mincing nothing about men and war,

About Heaven, and the work of fingers,

And the stars, and all that can be ordained—carving her *Amen*

As if into a broken tombstone (with the motto rasping

To live by assumptions is to let the world pass by).

I didn't want her to know I was watching

And tried to be curt, wrenish, sweet-smelling—

Part decoy, part misprisioner—

But she noticed me and the dumb jig.

So I said back to her: *Milk the cow that standeth still.*

And there we were—still, letting the world pass—

Then the afternoon tawnied into evening,

And the light webbed into the ground behind this motley wind,

And I decided that from then on I must study forgiveness

And truck with better wine and cut flowers.

That's when I thought of the cloud of crows

You'd told me about that grew silky over the rooftop

Bathsheba loved her king on—her king who touched her

As even he could not touch Goliath, touched her with the fingers

He used to write the psalms. The crows unwound

The sky from the wind like a cohort, precise as a name,

And yet no one figured their great love would ever be so revered.

ENGINE MAN

Part detonation and Elijahu,
Part foursquare and in *flagrante delicto*,

He's tepid, tepid, tepid.
Even at home, galled

And rummaged, a riot,
Or a rock, cuckolded,

If need be,
He's a thug of fidelity.

LITTLE CROW

—*For* W.

It lands flush with the virtue of an urge
And two winks, like a whip of thought—
Stung with an impulse, some *us*
And oncoming weeks of summer.
Though even this is akimbo,
Fluttering as morning flutters with false flowers.
Acorn-sweet, lightning's mate, star-crossed, downy,
Engraving the under-sky with mute fear,
It flies groggily into the heart's name,
The heart's law of terror,
Broken as a child, baroque as a lost color.

RAG AND BONE MAN

When he's grown old and removed the gothic armor,
Groomed his macho cogs into a moth's whisker,
He'll become less fictional and more fat—like a droopy
Canto with poor prosody—
A prudent endomorph, deposited and arch.
How many loved the cupid's dart he torched,
Caught between arc and circle, like a riderless tiger?
In truth, few loved—he was a prig and a jerk and a rake.
And all his *corpus juris* got bent to smack.
That business suit he wore—it was a subset
For bondage, efficient as a bunt,
Something he stubbed into himself, like a tune,
A crisp *huh*, an all-star rule, an autumn lust.
Neither prizefighter nor pig, seldom jealous
Or aled-up—he didn't know a spliff from a jailhouse.
His launch pad began with *mea culpa*—
Unpaunchy, glad-handed, marinated in aloe
And cups of lemon water. Therefore, he burrowed
Into dogma, bonded with orange dreams, and wooed.
If he could hop scotch through the epochs, bend
Toward echo and hope and prophecy,
He'd embargo the gnomes along with the grannies,
Plant a garden of blue weed, spritz his warts,
And think ugly about the girl from the launderette.

4

MAN AND WIFE

On this lousy road, among the last flowers, we are no better
Than eked-out fakes or harridans (we gave up
The dirt farm years ago). We've gotten good at browbeatings
And leaves of absence. We're slobbery as any rebutters,
Waylaid, yelling at the levelheaded. Inflamed, deformed,
We borrow the timetables for heaven. That's our devotion and
      our shield.
Whoever suspected that at night our right-of-way would lack carnage or
      caricature?
Instead, we simulate a circle of mystic laws
Like lewd Sabbaths—cuffed, radical, wagging and pulped
With our tawny rage, and no high jargon to get at the gimmickry.
We are as unavailing as lunatics. Our palaver has gone dry,
And gallivanting like nighthawks, we become in-and-outers, killers,
Mighty as dimes, stymied in the regular pickups of hash, routed,
Left unwinged, in the groan of the unfinished garden.

BLOOM AND DECAY

1

These twisted ivy patches are not a tale of pursuit, and any unraveling
That blinds us—rituals of envy, outlived slurs, old burns—
Has us stomaching odd moods that we get sick over but still obey.
If you silence the sky, my love, I'll close the boulevard down.
If you run hard in sleet and wind, then walk out of your life,
I'll stop at last in this city and die.

2

All evening now this city has been closer at hand and shinier—
The understory leaving us inseparable and maddened—
While the flinty candlelights in the window thin and canter,
Bloom and decay, and without question
Our eyes have opened to blackness and what is left unsaid:
This passage of delight is our sorrow and our bed.

THE HUMMINGBIRD

Today I studied pearls and fish and a procession of sheltered fowl,

Sang *Bone of My Bones* and danced to the tune that was played,

With and without a bride, with and without saints or seed.

Then the hummingbird landed in the feeder,

And like a summer of mime, it replenished the earth

With its red frown and ghostly bruise. I asked myself,

Could I cleave to luck or hoist sorrow into night

By a candle's flame? The ground was a fountain's spill

Of dozy swifts—as if we'd painted a garden of rapture

To bloody our hands. But we were resting

In the grass with your face to the sun and your knees bent,

And the dogwood ablaze with its pink scars—

I could have touched you as I touch a petal,

And all along your eyes alert and green and opened to grief.

If the arbor will give us shade to remember and forget,

Then we can loaf and watch the wingy light, and wait

For rain to carry the sky to us, and no longer beg for summer.

BATHSHEBA

When the unbroken dusk speckles into night,
And the wind drapes her up to the forbidden roof,
And the rains veil the doves, and the dogged minds
Shoulder their wheels of knowledge against the desert's pulpit,
Her mouth opens like a black sky, and the city's figs
Fall like the last charms and chambers of summer.
In this the cursed are anointed by her, purified, and fed.
While the heartbroken who fast in her presence are full of wishes.

How many strangers, though, insist at what gnaws at her
And demand she come home with their bliss-weary voices, calling:
Daughter of the oath, your bed is not a mound for orphans?
But her mind is whipped like sand.
Nightly: She flushes out silence and dotes on her children—
And on the king who has slept and wept beside her.

PSALM 51

Of tongues and offerings and *Before Me* sinners, what is left to say?

That there is always a tune in the gut that doffs fate?

That sacrifice is gracious, though all kindness gets broken?

That mercy is a sugar on the lips or an altar of guesses?

In the sun-swept places, we writhe,

Nose into shadows, grant that we've been crushed—

As if even today deliverance could be suspended from these woolly
     blossoms.

Now in the wingy twitter concealed as a heart is concealed,

We take our unpurified test and sleep lightly as dogs.

Say this: Of transcendence there is, some days at least,

A cup of cream, a window to stare through,

And a foreign city where nothing happens in sleep.

And this: Our blood and our hearts

Are gauzy as smoked glass. Surely we can name a star.

THE GREEN BED

Legendary things are gone now that once clanged
And glimmered in the good rooms and on faint stairs, learned
Things, told things—like stages of the moon.
Those first blushes between
Loves, hardly remembered, like hullabaloos,
Or the "hush, the children will hear," are edge-ways now, floral.
Here we've put the lamps out—though cannot quell
The zero-zone of what's frozen in us, and untouchable.
We hunt and count and lend garlands
And lacey things in the name of upright love—
And all the while, we become pundits on sleepy wives
Who claw in their own blood to prove their worth.
Then night comes on. We're reeled in and borrowed
And fall like shadows onto a green bed of praise
Or blame—two sorts of falderal we're unwise
To avoid, as if we could even avoid night when our minds
In sleep unfold into each other's quietest skin—
The terror never goes scot-free.
Nor is it a crow calling low in love that prances
On the wire in the half-swayed wind—a sign with no room for error.
The near light between the window-slats that veers
Into the lamentation of the sky, veers and masses on the all-damp road
And in the moony river, and your hand,
Wind-soaked and wound up,
Trafficking in foul goodness, from lips to lips,
Rises and falls across my spine. The newest day is here—
We whisper into our pillows about entering fear.

BANISHÈD

I said so little to myself. I said: *These nights are a siege.*
And: *The rudderless days are ghostly as a swan's eye.*
Then my mind painted a wide world
I could not see, though it seemed divine —
Like an island of free men braying,
And with the shores golden, and the moon like old wool.
Then my heart grew mysterious, quietly,
And sent me to the pit of glory closing upon joy,
Glory I could drum my eddied self into, like a whelp,
Glory longed for, worn through — and me dressed up
In a thought: *For hate's sake I spit my last breath at thee.*
The terms here are poison and purgatory,
The mind, like a confessor's,
Is full of scorn to cloak the body in,
And the lame hours melt inside my song of sin.

MARVEL

I did not call to the Holy Spirit or whistle *My lordy, lordy,*
Nor hum one scintilla of shame. What hid in the grass
Was neither skiver nor savior, neither cheater nor ace.
Besides, the doves peering over the gutters have all gone awry.
If I'm only a man, born far from a boomer's shack—
Hoarding sawbucks, cherry-picking the hicks like prey,
And the wusses, and the Horatian declaimers, and the lucky
Grubbers who master heartache and lurk like crooks
Among the rich and the rebadged—then I'm a rival devil,
Carrying my brag like a brakeman. And the one certainty,
That life is to be lost—and no matter the opinion, someone's
Always a fool—has me rubbed inside like a lonely breed
With the swill edgy and chic and rough. Who asks:
Who needs a cotton-eyed hymn to say what the old shanty
By the track has meant to the human story? Or:
What's Heaven for? The reach and grasp, the pecked-at days,
The horsey blues that lilac after hours,
The rocks I've carried in my coat pocket—
None of it has me shuddering on my knees.
Nevertheless, I marvel at the pigs and the ducks, at dogs and kings,
And revive this peck of flame, this tongue of lack, too easily.

SECRET

Forgive me: I was not at the guard station when I said I was.
Nor was I faithful to the near-hurt at first light when I washed
Like a concealed slave, keeping faith with my alleged self.
The slander was just so-so. As I saw it, the daisies off
In the choirmaster's mind were not anywhere near the crossroads
Or the labyrinths that sloped and unfurled in my head—
What with the stillness of fog still humped from the sleepless nights.
Or onioned, one said, adding, *Liars believe no one*. Safe
To say the call-back was: *To keep your mouth is to keep life*.
Besides, the guards were not accusers or the minister's wife.
Meanwhile, colliding like code, posturing with an austere snarl,
The secrets became canticles of rollick and quarrel
Then fitful as a child who scratches an elbow
Without consolation or creed or will.
The secrets secret from themselves. Finally, the morsels of it all:
Gossip separated friends; love like a crow stole
In on us; joy, the good silence of dirt and high clouds and grass;
And despair, cross-armed in the lamplight, cordial as the elements.

OVID IN EXILE

It's too late for superstition to erupt out of the micro-mercy
I putter around with in my head on nights in this room, shop-worn
As a purist, the sanity like a tiny nag from some other summer.
Today, the impropriety empties into a promise, the port-of-call
All rump and prey, and the far-off sunrise sprouting like an omen.
Each morning this spiky heat litters joy and reverses into nowhere.
Each afternoon, like snipes suddenly caught among the turnips—
I saw this once—the children in the courtyard pout toward supper,
And the mist from somewhere else stains the rinseless air—
And the semen I fear . . . well, all of it a bang-bang gamble.
Meanwhile, these yawning magnolias throb, like men, at dawn.
And the women grieve and get aroused and roam the city in wigs,
Vowing to be givers, grinning, smutty, as if put out to sea.
So much talk about veering and merging, and, on occasion,
Being a good fit for tea and bread, crimes and guilt.
Even from this room, with my body lanky and impish and ousted,
It's not hard to sag into the sulky opuses
With the dead-weight of whiskey and a regime of primness—
Call it, my new affirmation.
Still today, at last, without warning, autumn cut into the heat's skin
Like an overgrown harvest, the coolness gently sweeping
The lost summer into a mirror of communion.
Somewhere a dog barked deep inside my veins with half-sunk
     loneliness,
And the fields beyond the city went unplowed, and the sky tucked in
     tightly.
And finally, I imagined, un-strangled and gleaming into the sharp
     world,
Two boats, like incantations, cleared the open sea.

DISSOLUTION IN WINTER

There is neither light nor sleep between us now, the sun slicing,
Frail and flared, the room here all bonfire, the hard air
Strummed and sanctified, encroaching as a horizon—
And the bedrock we sat on once
Far from the salve for sorrow that must be patience.
You said: *Yesterday is a lost music, wedded to murder.*
Still, civility costs nothing: The poplars are one pleasure, one face of
      the deep.
When we were lithe as a city—igniting and sharp, unfenced,
Upright—our kitchen kettle whistled
Into the lavender rooms like an unassailed dream.
Then we were left to mull the last of our gardens
With the glory bower dying in the worn-over bed.
Then: Rat-eyed with it all, our bodies passed through each other.
And the sun drew its delicate light behind the trees.
And this morning, within earshot, rephrasing its awful *peep*,
One robin, without hesitation, deserted the snow-less branches.

O'BRYANT SQUARE

Like a little tincture of springtime in the dazzled day,
You were a sun-struck fugitive, tugging at creation
In the brick *platz*. All morning with the glare stirred up
And the unfinished war fought in the toughed-out distance,
The June city hunted us in its pink dress.
On the dry fountain's steps we sat like truants
As if sitting in a secret place
Where it was unbearable to see how ripped
The flurry of light was—
We thought we were licit and invisible.

Then a voice inside said: *Arise, come away,*
And wed the unworthiness to your cheeks, and sob
And squat and get queasy and turn wild and bitten back.
So we turned our backs on thoughts of sleep,
And our nerves were shrill, and shivered.
In that blaring sun, we were like children
Needing to act and unfold and serve fear.
We spoke of hope and woe and marriage,
But the day had to go on. Pompously, doomed,
We slumped off and ascended into our new lives.

THE THEORY OF HATS

It is hard even to admit this theory of hats, that to wear
The faithless one brimmed tightly over the eyes—
The featherless and discreet one, a hat with a secret code
That says, *To spoil the child is to fatten the serpent*—
To wear that hat (imperfectly as a crow's crown) against the sun
Is to bear the ruins of the unborn into our hearts—
He, shouting at the brunt of trees;
She, shifting like a seer to restore them.
It is hard to know happiness with a hat like that.
Or to forget the pangs sung with such burly impatience,
Or to heal the blurred things and soft hurts.
Even the blind self becomes a dervish, what with the torsion
And the far-off *vita nuova* like a new virus or virtuoso,
What with the tussles and old, pure-lit suppressions.
Then to be surprised by joy: Like the last rain of summer,
The big, spiraling, wounded animal of rain
With no place to turn, drumming the brown grass,
Rain falling without meaning, but perfectly faithful,
Into the petals of wind and the unopened roots—
Such tenderness looked to, like love, but unquestioned.
Then some afternoon with the sky lifting off again,
She will come to sit on the porch like a dark sparrow
And let the sun creep slowly onto her hair
And grow old and wonder about the balance of things.
And he beside her, sitting, too, distracted in the sun for hours,
But all the same, both of them, at last, so much warmer.

ACKNOWLEDGMENTS

I am grateful to the editors of the following periodicals for first publishing some of the poems in this volume:

Alaska Quarterly Review: "Embouchure"

The Grove Review: "Lust," "Old Adam Outside the Wall of Eden," "Overcast"

Hip Mama: "Bathsheba"

The Kenyon Review: "The Husband's Tale," "Ezra Pound," "The Wife's Tale"

Literary Imagination: "Secret," "Genesis 27"

The New Hampshire Review: "Kohain"

The New Republic: "Poet at Forty"

Oregon Humanities: "William Clark's Sonnets"

Perihelion: "The Sleeping Beauty"

Poetry: "Citizen Dave," "The Crooner," "Dover Butch," "Genesis 12," "Marvel," "Mass Man," "Mississippi God Damn," "Prudery," "Man and Wife" (as "Night Hawks"), "Rag and Bone Man," "Tale Bearer," "The Theory of Hats"

Portland Monthly: "P.O.E.M."

Seattle Review: "Banishèd," "Little Crow," "Ovid in Exile," "Psalm 51"

Slate: "Though Your Sins Be Scarlet"

Speakeasy: "Richard Hugo"

Windfall: "O'Bryant Square"

Alhambra Poetry Calendar 2008, edited by Shafiq Naz: "Genesis 12"

Alhambra Poetry Calendar 2009, edited by Shafiq Naz: "Dissolution in Winter"

Alhambra Poetry Calendar 2010, edited by Shafiq Naz: "The Hummingbird"

ABOUT THE POET

© Christine Rucker

David Biespiel was born in 1964 in Tulsa, Oklahoma, and grew up in Texas. His previous collections of poetry include *Wild Civility* and *Shattering Air*. He has been awarded a National Endowment for the Arts Fellowship in Literature, a Wallace Stegner Fellowship in Poetry, and a Lannan Fellowship, and he received the Pacific Northwest Booksellers award for editing the anthology *Long Journey: Contemporary Northwest Poets*. He has taught at many colleges and universities, including Stanford University and the University of Maryland, and currently divides his teaching among Oregon State University, Wake Forest University, and the M.F.A. Program at Pacific Lutheran University. Editor of *Poetry Northwest* and poetry columnist for the books section of *The Oregonian*, he is the founding director of the Attic Writers' Workshop in Portland, Oregon.

A NOTE ON THE TYPE

The poetry is set in 11 pt Electra with 18 pt leading. Electra, a modern face, was completed in 1935 by type designer William A. Dwiggins. It is highly legible and its italic—a true sloped roman—balances beautifully with the roman. Poem titles are set in FF Meta Bold 13 pt with 18 pt leading. FF Meta is a humanist sans serif typeface created in 1985 by Erik Spiekermann. The typesetting was done by Ashley Saleeba.